Deer Hunting for Beginners

The Ultimate Guide to Getting Started Hunting Deer: Tactics and Strategies for Tracking and Bagging Deer in North America

Jason Clark

All Rights Reserved. No part of this publication may be reproduced in any form or by any means, including scanning, photocopying, or otherwise without prior written permission of the copyright holder. Copyright © 2015

Table of Contents

Chapter 1 Introduction to Deer Hunting

Chapter 2 Hmm... Deer Meat

Chapter 3 Hunter Safety

- Selecting Your Weapon
- Three Rules for Gun Safety
- Rules to Bow Hunting
- Safety Courses
- Safety by Season

Chapter 4 Regulations and Sportsmanship

Chapter 5 Preparing Your Body for Hunting

- Top Five Exercises for Hunting
- Kick it into High Gear
- The Real Benefit of Fitness

Chapter 6 Knowing Your Weapon

- Weapons for Deer Hunting
- Selecting Your Cartridge
- Scopes

Chapter 7 Essential Equipment and Tools

Chapter 8 Ideal Hunting Times

- Time of Day
- Pressure
- The Moon
- The Rut

Chapter 9 Preparing for the Hunt

- Plan Ahead
- Check Your Gear
- Scouting the Field

- Start Practicing
- More on Preparation

Chapter 10 My First Trip

Chapter 11 Hunting Strategies

- Tips to Help You in Your Hunting Endeavors

Chapter 12 Taking the Shot

Chapter 13 Tracking the Deer

- Tracking a Healthy Deer
- Blood Tracking

Chapter 14 Packing it Back

- Tips for Dressing

Chapter 15 Recipes and Conclusion

Chapter 1 – Introduction to Deer Hunting

There's an addictive quality to hunting deer. It's true that deer hunting is not for everyone and many are turned off by the brutality of the sport. But for those of us who have fallen prey to the lure of hunting a large buck, the hook is substantial enough to make us forsake everything else in life when the time for hunting season comes.

The urge is from deep within and there is perhaps no greater outdoor activity for those who are ensnared in its culture, history, languages and myths.

For example, let's speak of the word *venison,* the lean meat of the deer. The word comes from the Roman word *Venus*, or the Goddess of love.

In other English terms, it comes from the word *venerate,* or to regard one with the deserved levels of respect. And yet another word it's often thought to be derived from is *venery,* which in its definition means the art of hunting as well as being in the pursuit of sexual pleasure. In any sense of the origins of the word, it's easily seen that it's associated with pleasure and power.

Regardless of the origins of the word venison, men and women all over the land have decided for one reason or another to take a shot at deer hunting. Many of the men and women who have decided to hunt deer come from a rural background, but this is not always the case, many also come from a busy city life and have decided to hunt with purpose for their meat rather than to choose the much easier route of convenience that comes with shopping at a super market or butcher store.

The motives for every hunter are different, for some it's a way to unplug from everyday life and take some much needed time to reconnect with nature. For others, it's the motivation that comes with imagining a nice cut venison steak or chops on the grill and the sweet and clean aroma and taste that will soon follow.

And yet there are still those who hunt for the thrill of the shot, the adrenaline that pumps through the body before taking down a large buck with the preferred method of "one shot, one kill," which is reminiscent of a Marine sniper's mantra.

Whatever an individual's motivation for deer hunting is, those who are new to the sport and lifestyle will find that locating a deer hunting guru is harder to do than one may think. Such is the reason for me creating this guide for deer hunting enthusiast like you. Whether you're an expert guide or a beginning shooter, this book will offer ways to help improve the hunt in every way possible.

There's no way for me to teach you everything you'll need to know, but I can help save you some time in preparation and methods. Sometimes however, you can't beat hands on experience when it comes to shooting.

There will be some of you who read this and absorb everything in a way that will help you bag a good buck on opening day, and for those of you who do, my hats off to you. You've gained my respect and envy, and probably that of your friends and family too. For most of you reading this however, the book will aid you and best be used in conjunction with the guidance of an experienced friend or relative.

What I aim for in this book is to help you from sounding like an idiot when you go hunting for your first time and to keep you from shooting yourself in the foot or your neighbor in his backside. Hopefully after reading this you'll also be able to best pick the people you want to hunt with and the ones you want to avoid being around while they have a gun.

Maybe you're wondering altogether if hunting deer is right for you and if that's the case in the next chapter I want to talk a little about the sport and some other aspects of it.

Chapter 2 – Hmmm Deer Meat...

I have a question for you. How many of you first time deer stalkers believe that deer hunting is the fastest route to an abundance of nearly free high quality all natural protein?

That's a good rationale when it comes to reasons for hunting deer, but if that's your only reason let me tell you something right now; you're better off buying a slab of beef or pork to get cheap meat. Deer meat is free, but it takes time to get for most people.

Unless you're a seasoned hunter, chances are it's going to be a while before you land a buck that feeds your family for the next year. But if you do bag a big one in your first year than get ready for the sweetest, most delicious, iron rich game on the planet. Deer meat is for the most part one of the healthiest meats you can find anywhere, as long as the deer are feeding on the right vegetation.

For most hunters however, it's going to be a decade or more of hunting to get the big kill. There will be plenty of substantial seasons and plenty of less than adequate one's, but that's all part of the fun.

The taste of a clean venison steak will make it all worth it though. The meat is packed full of the best nutrients like Iron and B Vitamins. Granted, beef and venison aren't that far off structurally, but the way they are raised has everything to do with the quality of the meat.

Venison is oftentimes flavored by the feed that the deer eat. Sage gives its own distinct flavor vs. that of basil or verbena. This is why deer from different regions have different flavors. They are all unique and all delicious, typically however, only the most experienced hunters will notice the difference.

As a last word of warning, pregnant women should be careful when eating deer, it's rare, but if a deer has been shot by lead based ammunition in the past there is a chance that the meat could result in lead poisoning.

Now that we've spoken a little bit about the benefits of eating deer meat, let's move on to what you're really here for, hunting. Before we go off into hunting strategies though, we need to talk about safety, it's the most important aspect of hunting.

Chapter 3 – Hunters Safety

Out of all the tough sports in the world, hunting is by far one of the most dangerous. Hunting isn't just dangerous because of the gun; hunting is dangerous because of the improper handling and use of the gun by inexperienced hunters.

Since a hunter is responsible for the safety of himself and the people around him or her, there are several safety measures which need to be taken to guarantee that everyone remains safe. Safety can't be emphasized enough, it's not just danger that could occur or injury, but people's lives are at stake, hence why I've devoted an entire chapter to safety.

IMPORTANT SIDE NOTE: All hunters should use this chapter as a guideline and reminder only. It's recommended that all hunters pass a hunters safety course before actually partaking in any shooting or hunting.

As for this chapter there are several areas which we should touch on in regards to hunter's safety, and they are as follows:

- **Hunting Equipment (More on this in later chapters)**
- **Gun Safety**
- **Bow Safety**
- **Hunting Safety Courses**
- **Seasonal Hunting Safety**

One of the biggest aspects of hunting is choosing the right weapon for the job and all its related supplies. Whether you're going hunting with a gun or a bow it doesn't matter, both are dangerous and should be respected as such.

Selecting Your Weapon

When you're going deer hunting you need to first select the appropriate gun or bow for your trip. For example, a typical pistol would not be considered appropriate for deer while a crossbow or rifle would be. On the other hand taking a moose hunting rifle would be wrong for deer as the gun is simply too powerful.

Aside from selecting the right weapon for the job, another important factor is to make sure that your weapon is taken care of properly. This means to make sure that it's cleaned and operating correctly. Once you've selected your weapon there are some general rules.

Three Rules to Gun Safety

The first rule is to always check to see if your gun is loaded in the appropriate and safe fashion when you first pick it up. And never under any means look down the barrel, this may sound obvious, but people make dumb mistakes from time to time.

The second rule of hunter's safety is that that the safety feature should always be on the weapon unless you're preparing to shoot at your prey.

The third rule of hunters safety is you should never point your gun towards anything or anyone you don't intend on shooting. You must be aware of where the muzzle of your weapon is at all times and never point it at your own feet.

Taking a round to the foot is extremely uncomfortable at best, and can actually be one of the worst experiences a person can go through. Not to mention it oftentimes requires a series of surgeries to repair all of the bones and tendons.

It's important to remember that this rule applies regardless of whether or not the weapon is loaded / unloaded or the safety is on or off. The reason this is such an important rule is that if the gun should accidently go off, it's better to misfire into nothing than into a fellow hunter.

Rules to Bow Hunting

Hunting with a bow takes a tremendous amount of strength, skill and energy. There are just as many rules if not more that a hunter needs to take into consideration when bow hunting.

The first rule is to make sure you check your bow before you leave for your hunt. If there are any strings or wires that are frayed or damaged then you need to replace them before going into the field. A snapped string can cause welts or cuts which are usually minor, but it can take serious time to fix in the field and is best taken care of at base camp or home.

Second rule of bow hunting is to use the correct arm protection or guards. You will want to wear them when you notch your arrow and are preparing to make the kill. Arm guards will help protect you if a wire should snap.

The third rule is to keep in mind that you have a bow that you can actually use, or in other words make sure your bow matches your own strength. It's true that being able to use a heavier bow is big for bragging rights, but pulling a bow that is too strong for you can cause severe and very painful injuries that take serious time to heal. If you must use a heavier bow to kill deer than you should work up to it, this can help to avoid strains and muscle damage from taking a shot.

Hunting Safety Courses

Before you head out for your first trip, make sure you take your local hunting course. Even if you're a seasoned hunter and shooter but you haven't been hunting in some time, it's a good idea to take advantage of safety classes to refresh your skills and knowledge.

Safety courses cover everything from proper handling as well as covering local hunting laws in your area; you should be well educated in all the local laws before you go hunting. The classes are even a good idea for anyone who doesn't hunt but lives in an area which is frequented by hunters.

Hunting Safety by Season

In some areas, like those with thick brush, vegetation, or which are heavily forested, hunting safety is something to always keep in mind. Since there are so many hunters out in force during each of the specific seasons, you should always make sure and be aware that you're wearing clothing appropriate to the area and the season. Bright clothing works best like oranges which are easiest for people to see but still hidden from deer since they see in black and white.

Wearing appropriate clothing is important whether you're a hunter or a non-hunter in the area and especially if you're on someone else's property. Make sure that you always have permission from the land owner when you are going to hunt on someone else's property, and if possible inform them when you plan on being on/off their property.

It is important to obtain permission, because every land owner is different and some may not give you access to their lands. Some owners have no trespassing signs, while others are more than happy to let hunters come. If you're given permission, keep in mind that you need to be observant when it comes to the people living on that property, especially children and animals.

Keep all of these tips in mind and you shouldn't have any issues with hunting and safety. The most important factor of hunting is to keep you and others out of risk of injury or death. Knowing the safety rules and being educated can be the difference between a good hunt and a trip to the hospital or morgue. Now that you know about hunting safety, let's get on with a little more of the important stuff before getting into hunting and hunting preparation. The next chapter will be on hunting regulations and proper sportsmanship.

Chapter 4 – Regulations and Sportsmanship

When it comes to regulations, it's going to be on a state basis so this will only be some generalized guidelines for hunters everywhere. For the most part the regulations are going to refer to hunting times, bag limits, deer sizes and weapons allowed.

There are some other important factors to consider as well for all of us. Hunting is a privilege that we get as Americans. And it's each state and its officials that welcome hunters to the local fields and forest to hunt deer. Here's the thing though, people oftentimes get overly excited and fail to comply with local law.

We get excited the first time we take our children hunting and get to see them bag their first deer. We get to experience the thrill of tracking and the adrenaline leading up to the shot. We get the rush of excitement when we get a clean kill, and the stories that follow a long treck back to base camp and eventually home.

The entire experience is perhaps one of the greatest on earth and we get excited to do it all again the next year. The excitement can make some people forget about proper conduct and sportsmanship.

Every ecosystem is a balanced source of flora and fauna. In our hunting trips we get to see all types of wildlife like duck and geese, or even badgers in some areas. It's important that we respect the local habitat and only go for our kill, it's also important that we leave it as it was when we came.

It's respect for the local land and laws by all of us that will keep the areas open for the future hunters of America.

Even many private land owners don't have a problem with "guests" hunting on their lands as long as they're clean, safe, and respectful to the landowner. Basically, it comes down to treating the land like it was your own and the landowner like you would like to be treated. It also means to understand the local laws and regulations that are going to vary from state to state and county to county.

Now that we've touched on regulations, let's talk about how to avoid being "that guy" by practicing good sportsmanship.

Before we begin, there is something very important that I want to speak about, and it could have been put in the hunter's safety section, but I decided to put this important rule here as it applies to the safety and wellbeing of everyone in the area which is what sportsmanship is really about. And that rule is that alcohol, drugs, and guns don't mix.

The rule of no substances with guns is respected by all real hunters and gun enthusiast and is non-negotiable. Sobriety is an important fundamental part of hunting and this means no drinking until five AM and then picking up your rifle and heading out the door. People's lives are on the line and clarity is a must for the true hunter.

Okay moving on, there's an old expression that goes "That person is a good sport." That means they follow good practices and obey the general rules that apply to the respected game. Typically, a person who is a good sport is someone who is friendly, happy, and always willing to help out when it's needed.

On the other hand we have a "bad sport." The bad sport takes unfair advantages of other people and will cheat to get the advantage. Typically the bad sport is negative and generally unsafe.

While "bad sports" may be harmless in t-ball, there is zero tolerance for them in deer hunting. It doesn't matter if they're hunting with a bow, shotgun, rifle or muzzleloader, when you hunt you take full responsibility for everything and if you're not going into the field with other peoples best interest in mind then stay at home.

Being a good hunter takes skill, basic knowledge of local laws, wildlife, and the area you're in as well as a good attitude. NEVER HUNT WITH A PERSON WHO IS UNSPORTSMANLIKE!

As stated before, each area will have its own laws which can be studied and learned from the proper authorities, online, and through the use of pamphlets wherever licenses are sold.

There is however, other ethical rules of conduct which are unwritten and followed by the true sportsman. Writing them all down isn't easy, but here are some examples below:

- It may not be illegal to take a shot who is clearly someone else's. But no real sportsman would every take a shot from someone else.

- It may not be illegal to hog all the shots from other hunters. But no real sportsman would ever take all the shots.

- It may not be illegal to fire a weapon which hasn't been properly sighted. But no real sportsman would ever head into the field with an inadequately sighted weapon.

Each of the above actions are considered to be perfectly legal, but a real sportsman would never perform any of them. Real hunters and sportsmen don't need written laws for every code of conduct and stay within safe practice and ethical boundaries. Real sportsmen follow and obey all of the unspoken rules and laws anyway. Following the written and unwritten laws is the main difference between sportsman and unsportsmanlike attitude and behavior.

Most of you are just starting your career as hunters and no one expects you to know everything that is happening at all times. The important trait to develop is the use of common sense, good judgement and continual learning of skills and regulations. This applies to everyone and will help keep the hunting fields safe.

Now on to chapter five, preparing your body for hunting, because this is not a sport for the feint or week bodied individual.

Chapter 5 – Preparing Your Body for Hunting

Being in shape is crucial to successful deer hunting. Let's say you only have a few months to get in shape for the big hunt though, can you go from a beer drinking couch potato to a lean mean deer hunting machine in only three months? Yes you can, with the right plan, proper motivation and commitment you can get in considerable shape in just 90 days.

I can give you a plan and tell you how to motivate yourself but it's really going to be up to you. The hardest part of any fitness regime is getting started and making it a habit. You will also need to develop a routine that isn't overwhelming or too brutal to keep you going.

There's no right answer as to which is best, weightlifting, jogging or biking. I find that a balanced regime is going to serve you best and since you're getting in shape for deer hunting, it makes sense to also do hiking as well. It's most important that you do something, doing anything will always be better than doing nothing. Let's talk about why you getting off your butt is so important for hunting to begin with.

Motivation to All Hunters

Most hunters in the field will find their greatest success when they can use all of their effort effectively. Being able to push on when everyone else is tired and worn out will more often than not result in a kill at the end of a hunt.

Hunting with enthusiasm and perseverance almost always pays off. The hunters who can give forth the fullest effort from the time they lace their boots up until the end of the day are usually the individuals who will get the monster buck. The advantages of fitness aren't just for the benefit of increased hunting odds; it also makes you tough and creates confidence, even if you are just sitting up in a tree stand.

The major mistake is when hunters rush out firing after only a few days of improper preparation, they end up getting mentally, emotionally, and physically exhausted which can lead to quitting. It's much better to spend a few months instead in preparation for the big hunt.

The following is a schedule you can follow as a guideline to help you get in better shape for hunting

In the first 1-4 weeks it's important to build a solid foundation. Keep your eyes focused on the bigger picture and take small steps towards your goal of being a physically fit hunting machine. Your current level of fitness is also going to have a lot to do with how you begin your fitness regime.

In any case, start slowly with just 30 minutes a day of walking or jogging. You may have to get up earlier, go during lunch, or just after putting the kids to bed. Taking some type of action is what's most important, after that you will want to turn the action into a habit by performing it for 21 days.

How much you do isn't as important as making sure that you're pushing yourself. By pushing yourself and focusing on form you will build a solid foundation which the rest of your fitness can be built on.

Diet is another important part of fitness; you will have to stay clear of beer and fast food for a while. Start off eating whole grains or oatmeal for breakfast. Follow up later meals with lean proteins like venison, turkey, fish, and nuts. Eat a lot of vegetables and some fruits as well as drink plenty of water. Stick to the diet all the way up to the hunt and you'll watch the pounds fall off.

For the sake of guidance, I will give you some easy exercises you can use to help get in shape as well. They are mainly focused on legs and core which will give you the best results in the field.

Top Five Exercises for Hunting

Squats – Good for lower back, core and legs. Make sure and study form and start with lightweights to see what you can handle. If you do these exercises right you can transform your body and if you do them wrong you'll just hurt yourself.

Military Press – Using dumbbells works best and these work well for the core and upper body. Make sure to use proper form and get a spotter if you need to keep things safe.

Lunges – Mostly for the legs, these also are good for the core as well. Make sure and do both legs an equal amount of times and use a barbell with light weights for added effect.

Pull Ups – Most people hate this exercise because you can't fake them. Make sure you perform a full range of motion and start small. Try different grips and positions for working different muscles.

Cleans – You could do only this and get in amazing shape. Watch videos to get the form with this move as it is very easy to hurt yourself.

Kick it into High Gear

After you've performed the following for a month or so it's important to increase your intensity to improve your gains. You can also add high intensity interval training at this point with sprints or kettle belles. The important idea I want to get across to you is that you want to continually push yourself and if your workout is getting easy step it up a notch.

The last weeks leading up to your hunting trip should be fun. You'll be seeing results by now as long as you've stayed committed to your fitness. Keep pushing yourself and eating healthy and you'll be a monster ready for the kill and the hunt.

The Real Benefit of Fitness

Throughout the years I've seen plenty of men and women push themselves to get in shape. And what happens during the physical transformation is incredible. The discipline and confidence spills into every area of their life including hunting. They are able to push themselves when the time comes and get the big game that most people will never see.

Not to mention that when the time comes to pack the deer out, you have a serious advantage when compared to the guy who can't even bend over to tie his shoelaces.

Chapter 6 – Knowing Your Weapon

As hunting season closes in, hopefully you have a weapon already. If you know your gun and have been hunting for years you can read this chapter or continue on. For the rest of you, your weapon is an extension of you and the way you kill your deer, so read this chapter carefully before selecting your gun.

There are different weapons to select from when hunting. And the following are some of the varieties you have to select from.

Weapons for Deer Hunting

Bow/Crossbow – Picking the right bow can be a challenge. You'll want to identify accuracy, draw length, and draw weight, total mass, arrow speed, bolt length and color. Each of these will help to determine the bow you purchase.

Remember that in addition to the bow you will have the quiver of arrows as well. When selecting a bow you want to select one which is comfortable for you to handle. A steady aim is required when firing a bow and if you select a bow which is too heavy for you it will prove to be disastrous in your hunting attempts.

The more stable and steady you are the less movement there will be for the deer to see. Weighted stabilizers are available to help with movement as well. When selecting a crossbow the main difference is going to be in weight distribution, but for the most part the same rules apply.

Pistol – I only put this in here because I'm sure many of you have questions about pistols and deer hunting. Unless you're a skilled shooter and have put your time in with practice, don't use a pistol. Handguns take considerable skill and marksmanship to get the standard "one shot, one kill."

An inexperienced shooter will oftentimes miss by a couple of inches which will either injure the animal temporarily or make the kill take considerable time. In either case it goes against proper ethics of good sportsmanship. If you have a desire to hunt with pistols, most use a .22 caliber because of their accuracy, but you will have to do your own investigation into which type of handgun to shoot with and what locations allow you to hunt with them.

Shotgun – Not as commonly used as rifles, although some states make it almost a necessity to hunt with shotguns, they are similar to rifles in their actions. Pump is the most commonly used action with shotguns and the most reliable.

Where shotguns differ is in their ammunition types. Shotgun ammunition is measured in gauges. 12 gauge is the most common although they do come in 20, 10 and 410 as well. Gauges are the size of the round and the smaller the gauge the larger the round.

After selecting the type of round, you will want to select the chamber. There are three options: 2 ¾, 3, and 3 ¾ inch. The chamber refers to the length of the shell. A shotgun which is chambered for 3 ¾" is the most versatile as it can fire all of the other lengths as well.

When hunting deer with a shotgun you will want to use slugs or load. The traditional scatter shot is not effective for deer hunting and will damage the meat.

Muzzleloader – This is another weapon type like the pistol that I will not go into detail about. The reason being is that muzzle loaders are best left to the experts as well. A muzzleloader is a rifle type which is front loaded with wad, powder and then bullet.

They take considerable skill and for those of you are who are new to hunting I recommend if you truly desire to use muzzleloaders to speak with a hunter who is specialized in using these traditional types of firearms.

Rifle – By far the most widely used weapon when deer hunting, there is a lot that goes into selecting the right rifle. To start your selection in an intelligent manner you first have to select the cartridge size.

For most people's purposes there are four very common cartridge sizes:

- .270 Winchester
- .308 Winchester
- 30-06 Springfield
- .300 Winchester Magnum

All of the above are acceptable deer hunting cartridge sizes and will get the job done. To safely fire a cartridge it MUST be in the appropriate rifle type.

After Selecting Your Cartridge

The following are other aspects that go into selecting a hunting rifle.

- **Action Type –** This is how the cartridge is moved from the storage location to the chamber. The four types of actions are bolt action, pump action, lever action and self-loading.

  Bolt action is the simplest and most dependable, and the most commonly used of all the action types.

- **Stock Materials –** Wood, fiberglass, plastic, and laminated wood are all different types of stocks available. Different types of stocks change the weight of the rifle, its balance, and the price. They are also responsible for the look and feeling of the gun.

- **Barrel Length –** Barrel lengths are usually from 18"-26" and not all lengths are available on all models of guns. Barrel length effects stiffness of the barrel, the weight of the weapon, the rifle length, and the speed that the bulled leaves the barrel (AKA muzzle velocity).

  Typically shorter barrels are a bit more accurate as they don't wiggle the rifle so much. But when it comes to hunting a little accuracy lost can have a dramatic effect.

On the other hand, the longer bullets tend to have a higher muzzle velocity as the gas behind the bullet has a longer length of time to push the bullet forward.

- **Metals and Finishes** – Last and not least is the finish of the rifle. Available materials are usually carbon and stainless steel. Carbon is cheaper but will rust at a faster rate. And after selecting the type of metal there are different finishes for each. The finishes are typically "bluing" and "stainless."

Scopes

Next to your rifle, a scope is the only other item which is essential to hunting deer. Buying a scope has changed dramatically in the last few decades, where you could once count on a Weaver for budget, or a Lyman or Leupold when you were well off, now there are endless amounts of scopes on the market which you can choose from.

There are some rules when you are selecting a scope that apply

1. Avoid scopes which make you sound funny when you pronounce their name.

2. You don't have to spend an arm and a leg to get a good scope. You can good scopes for $200-$300.

3. The most overrated quality with scopes is brightness. While brightness is important, there isn't a scope

available on the public market which will let you shoot from first to last legal light.

4. A scope's primary attribute should be its toughness. It needs to hold up to the elements, hiking, being smashed and beat up.

5. Power is the next most important feature of a scope. AKA its sharpness, you should be able to pick out a brown deer hide on a grey surface.

6. Avoid buying complicated scopes, you only need the basics and buying a complicated scope will cause issues in time.

7. When you're hunting deer you don't need anything too crazy or over 10X. A 1X-4X is ideal or the popular 3X-9X is also a good option.

8. Never buy a scope that is shiny. Shiny scopes scream "run" to the deer you are trying to shoot.

The Bottom Line When Selecting Your Weapon of Choice

It's going to be your final decision on what you hunt with. I suggest before you buy anything you head to a shooting range and try different rifle types to see which best suits you. You can also ask friends and family who are hunters to try their guns out and see which you like best.

Read on for more, in the next chapter we will discuss in detail equipment and tools that are necessities.

Chapter 7 – Essential Equipment and Tools

Throughout the years deer hunting has evolved and changed. What people used to take hunting are now left behind or forgotten and replaced with new items. Most of us who hunt can agree that rarely is a hunting pack as light as you'd like it to be, but it's never filled with anything that isn't going to be used.

Below is a List of Items You Don't Want to Forget on Your Hunt – I left out the gun, ammo and scope for obvious reasons

1. **Hunting Pack** – Your hunting pack is where you keep all of your hunting goodies and tools. You can use whatever color you like but I always use camouflage of some type. Get the right backpack and it can last you a lifetime, you may have to sew it up every now and then but you'll grow to love it. The best suggestion is to find one which is best suited for you and your needs. Once you find the right pack you'll stick with it and it will serve you well.

2. **Compass** – Anyone who goes in the woods should have a compass whether they're hunting or not. They should also be able to read that compass and know which direction will lead out if they get turned around or lost. GPS units are great but are no substitutes for an old school magnetic compass that doesn't run off batteries and works no matter where you're at.

3. **Water** – A definite must have, water can be used to drink, clean wounds, clean hands after field dressing your kill and the bottle can be used for pee once it's gone. Just don't pee in your favorite water bottle.

4. **Light Rope or Heavy Cord** – This is one of the most versatile and useful pieces of equipment available and can be used for more uses than you realize. You can use it for everything from securing things to your tree stand, making a temporary rifle sling, or to help drag a killed deer. Keep at least one in your pack at all times.

5. **Knife** – Old timers never left home without a knife and you should never go hunting without one. You should be able to get to your knife fast and efficiently, I always like to keep a knife handy on me and another one in my pack for safety measures.

6. **Lighter and Matches** – Lighters are good for several reasons, you can burn items to check wind direction, melt any thread hanging off your clothing and starting a fire in an emergency. Matches are good to have around as well.

7. **Flashlight** – Going into the woods without a flashlight is the same as going without a knife, it just doesn't make sense. They're handy for finding your way to your stand or back to camp. Flashlights are also handy when you need to get into your pack for one reason or another. Make sure and keep your light handy.

8. **Saw and Pruner** – These are essential for clearing brush and other obstructions from your line of sight. Small folding saws always work well as do pruning shears for smaller items.

9. **Toilet Paper** – Sometimes the call of the wild happens and when you gotta go, you gotta go. The last thing you want to do is wipe your butt with poison ivy. Make sure you burry your used paper so no one steps in it. TP also works well for wiping off face paint and creating a trail if you're blood tracking an animal.

10. **Grunt and Bleat Calls** – Calls don't always work, but when they do it is well worth the time and energy it takes to perform them. I don't ever head into the field without one of these babies.

11. **Gloves or Glomitts** – During warmer weather I always recommend lighter weight gloves. Gloves help to hide your hands, and when it's cold out they keep you warm. Glomitts are perfect for hunting; they are the fingerless gloves which have mitten pockets which can fold over to keep your hands warm.

12. **Mask/Camo Makeup Face Paint** – When you're hunting it's important to stay concealed. Oftentimes the number one reason that a hunter is foiled is because they are seen or heard. You can still bag a deer if you're seen, but it's going to be a lot tougher. Dark paint is therefore important to keeping your face hidden. You can use

either face paint or makeup to stay hidden. It's entirely up to you.

13. **Spare Batteries** – Make sure you bring some spare batteries for whatever electronics you have. Getting caught out in the woods with dead batteries is one of the most irritating experiences and the sign of a true rookie.

14. **Pee Bottle** – Deer don't like the scent of urine unless it's other deer. Peeing in the woods won't hurt anything but the scent may be enough to deter your prey from showing up in your area.

15. **Scent Killer** – It's impossible to hide all of your smell, but scent killer can be a good way to dull it down. It's especially important if you're hiking a lot and there is a ton of sweat. It may be 100% effective but it's worth using if it will land you a large buck.

16. **Flagging Ribbon or Surveyor's Tape** – This works well for making trails and marking killed animals. It also works well marking a trail from your stand to your car or truck.

17. **Spare Ammo/Arrows** – I know I mentioned this before, but I am going to do it again. Make sure you have spare ammo, arrows and arrowheads.

18. **GPS Unit** – Some of you may be able to live without a GPS unit, I know I can. But I don't really like too. I like to mark each stand location and set it as a waypoint. I also

use it to mark other things in the area like roads and trails and other like objects. It works well if you're searching for a deer which has been shot and you have to make search patterns.

That pretty much sums up this chapter, if you're camping then you should know what you need to bring with you, if not buy a book on camping.

Other than that you're going to have to play around to see what you want and don't want to bring with you but this is just a guideline of sorts.

The next chapter is going to be on the best times to go hunting.

Chapter 8 – Ideal Hunting Times

Timing is always taken into consideration by hunters as a necessity. Hunters have to make efficient use of their free time to plan hunting trips. They have to deal with an already busy life and still make time to hunt the deer in the most effective manner.

When it comes to deer specific times, specific days, certain weeks and even different months can contribute to the success of a hunter. There are several different variables which have to be taken into account.

Time of Day

Both deer hunters and research can tell you that deer are crepuscular or not active at dawn and dusk. This is extremely true in the beginning of a season. When you hunt close to home it's a bit easier as you can get in an hour or so before you head off to work without missing any action.

Pressure

If you're hunting on heavily populated public land than you have a couple of different options, the first is to hunt weekdays when most the crowds will be at work. Even Mondays and Fridays aren't great days to hunt so you may want to hunt closer to the middle of the week. The second option is to let the pressure of crowds work for you by letting the people move the deer for you while you sit back in the thick.

The Moon

Research was performed by North Carolina State University which shed some new light on how the moon effects the deer movement. The study showed that deer performed a majority of their movement during the hours of twilight. The research showed that hunters who follow the phase of the moon and hunt during twilight hours may be at a slight advantage.

The Rut

Most of the states have reported that rut dates are very similar year to year. They're also fairly synchronous from the mid of the continent to the north of the continent. Peak breeding is typically reported to be around mid-November. It's important as a hunter that you understand the difference between peak rut and peak breeding periods. Bucks are always more active a week to a week and a half prior to peak breeding. Once the does are in estrous, most of the bucks will be in hiding and the woods suddenly become a very desolate place to be.

Final Thoughts on Timing

There isn't much else that can be said about timing except that it's up to you to determine the best hunting times in your area. You can head online and find several websites with charts that will show you everything you need to know about proper hunting times in your area. Another great piece of advice is to find a local hunter; they'll be able to best tell you the behavior of deer in the area.

Alright, so you've read through all this now it's time to get out in the field. The next chapter will be preparing for the hunt; it's time to let the fun begin.

Chapter 9 – Preparing For the Hunt

Don't just go running out to start hunting without preparation. I know you've been reading this to get prepared, but there are still a few more bases to cover which I will go over in this chapter. They're important and I'll keep the chapter relatively short.

Below Are 25 Ideas to Help You Get Prepared for Your Hunt

Plan Ahead

1. **Start by setting the plan early for the upcoming season** – Where are you hunting? When will you be going and who will you be going with?

2. **Are there new hunters going hunting with you** – If you have new hunters joining you, make sure they have completed their safety course and read this book.

3. **Are you an experienced hunter** – If so make sure and have your hunter education card ready for opening day of hunting season.

4. **Hunting Licenses** – It's important that everyone who will be hunting has up to date hunting licenses so you are current with all the local laws.

5. **Regulations and Laws** – Make sure that everyone you take hunting with you knows the local laws and regulations, not just one of you.

Check Your Gear

1. **Condition** – Get all of your gear together and see what is in need of repairing or replacing.

2. **Research** – Go online and find out what gear is new or improved on the various websites. There could be something that helps you land the big buck or pack him home after the kill.

3. **Go to the local hunting shops** – You may be able to find discounted items for the upcoming hunting season or other new gear you can check out in person.

4. **Clothing** – Replace or repair damaged clothing you need to take with you.

5. **Research Online** – Get online and find out what other hunters are saying in your area. There may be some great tips out there that can help you.

6. **Buy ammunition** – It's important to stock up on ammo ahead of time since the shelves tend to get cleared out pretty quick when the season gets close or has already started.

7. **Replace blades** – If you're a bow hunter put on new blades on broad heads.

8. **Arrows** – Check your arrows for damage and replace or repair as needed.

9. **Clothing** – Try on your hunting camouflage to make sure that it fits properly and break in new clothing before the season begins.

Scouting the Field

1. **Landowners** – Start knocking on doors and asking for permission to hunt on their property if need be.

2. **Scouting** – Begin watching and scouting for deer in the area if it is public property or private property which you have the permission to hunt on.

3. **Gratitude** – If you asked someone for permission to hunt on their land and they have said yes, then make sure you give them a gift to show gratitude.

4. **Trails** – Start finding the game trails that are used and searching for scat to begin analyzing their movements.

5. **Stands** – It's time to start thinking about where you will place your stand with the information you've gathered from your scouting.

6. **Cameras** – If you have cameras start placing them so you can check to see what type of deer are in the area and what they look like.

Start Practicing

1. **Shooting** – Get your tail to the range or property and start pulling the trigger on that gun or the drawstring on that bow.

2. **Sighting** – Check the sighting of your bow or rifle and adjust it as needed to get accuracy.

3. **Knives** – Sharpen your knives and study cuts and cleaning procedures if you need too. Clean dressing of your kill is an important aspect of the hunt.

4. **Get Pumped** – It's almost time for the hunt so start watching your favorite hunting shows or watching old videos and get excited for the season that's about to start.

5. **Enjoy the hunt** – Be safe and get a big one!

More on Preparation

On average, 26% of all deer-hunters head into the hunting field with their friends and family. Make sure that anyone you're going hunting with is prepared as well. It only takes one bad apple to ruin the bunch. And if you have young ones who you want to take hunting with you in the future, it may be a good idea to take them in the field with you even if they won't be hunting so they can get used to hunting practices. Just make sure to be safe and intelligent!

Are you getting excited yet? You should be because the next chapter is on basic hunting strategies.

Chapter 10 – My First Trip

Maybe you didn't grow up hunting; maybe you've only hunted duck and fowl. Maybe you're in your 30's and don't know where to begin. It's all good though; it's never too late to start hunting and once you get the feeling for hunting you'll love it. It will get in your blood and along with the hunting you'll love the culture.

I remember the first time I went big game hunting I was in my 20's and I had been hunting duck and a few times and turkey for a number of years.

A friend invited me to go hunting and I loved it. The campfire camaraderie and everything else that went with hunting deer was right up my alley. I was angry I hadn't started sooner in life but I decide to make up for lost time.

Something definitely awakened within me that trip. After that I couldn't do anything but think about hunting. I was warned that getting overzealous was dangerous and not to get too excited. My friends and old timers all said that many people go years without ever landing a big buck or even seeing one.

"Fine, I understand," I would say.

But regardless of all that I wanted to increase my chances of getting a big one. And with the next season drawing near a couple of major problems came up. My friend who was supposed to go had a wedding to attend.

We were upset to say the least; we had spent a lot of time in preparation getting gear ready. We would take trips to base camp whenever possible and work on that, building tree stands, putting up cameras, and scouting the area. I had done all my research on my rifle and gotten in the best shape of my life. All the gear was ready for the hunt and so where we, so this wedding threw a cog in the wheel.

And on top of that, my other friend had a family emergency that came up. It looked as if our entire trip was going to get cancelled. Then I thought I don't need those guys I'll go alone.

So I did.

When Saturday came I got up. I packed and hit the road at about 3:30 in the morning to make the two hour drive and give myself plenty of time to get to my stand. The stand wasn't the best but it worked, and after all the preparation I was finally hear for my first solo deer hunt. I was ecstatic and hungry for a kill.

I kid you not, just twenty minutes into the hunt I saw my first deer and she was big. She came running through and my blood was pumping. Seeing the deer was a great experience to say the least.

After an hour or so, I realized that my butt wasn't the best seat in the house and it wasn't meant for hours on end of being planted on a cold wooden stand. I had not thought to bring a cushion or small chair (first tip).

With my back and butt aching in pain I moved. I stretched but it didn't help. I mumbled under my breath about how much I hated my stand and how I would invest in cushion, dropping curse words here and there.

It was about an hour and twenty minutes later that I saw a huge deer. A very big doe, it was awesome but there was no doe season so I just watched. She moved behind a tree and I lifted my rifle so I could get a closer look and then it hit me.

As "she" lifter her head I saw the two little bumps. This was a buck and the little bumps where tiny, about the size of the tip of your finger.

My rifle was sighted 2.5" high for 100 yards with the best ammo so I was all good to take the shot. The funny thing was that the buck was only about 50 ft. away. And after I shot I'm pretty sure the sound gave it a heart attack before the bullet did the job.

I had killed my first deer...

I couldn't believe it; I really killed a deer in just a few hours of my first solo trip. He may not have had the rack I was looking for but he was a good sized buck none the less. It seemed so simple to me and I couldn't realize why everyone had been so forthcoming about warning me about being patient. It was simple, wait, shoot, get deer, and go home.

This is where my deer education began. All the interviews and videos I had watched couldn't prepare me for what was about to happen. Over the next five hours I learned a lot and now I will share what I learned.

Below are the lessons I can share for you from a beginner deer hunter (at the time)

- Deer are heavy.

- Deer get heavier when they die. This doesn't make sense of seam practical, but there is no way this thing could have weighed this when it was alive. I'm pretty sure this is where the term dead weight comes from.

- There's no good place to hold on to a dead deer without antlers. Dragging the animal by its legs is next to useless and near impossible. Even without antlers the head gets caught up on everything.

- DO NOT grab the tarsal glands. These are the glands on the inside of the legs where the buck urinates to keep scent. Yes I grabbed there and it haunts me to this day.

- Tarsal gland scent never goes away. The skin has to die and fall away before your hands stop smelling.

- When you're dragging the deer back to camp be prepared for a long walk. It may only be a half mile from base camp, but by the time you get back it will feel like ten.

- Mud makes the deer heavier and adds to the tendency to drag.

- It will take you hours to drag a deer out by yourself even if it's only a half mile. For me it was about two and a half.

- Gut the deer immediately. Within just a few hours after death, the bowel gas will "come out" upon gutting and trust me it's about as bad as the tarsal gland scent.

- If it's your first time hunting, you're going to get angry at this point when you call your friends for advice and they laugh at you.

- Your first solo deer will be dirty after cleaning it and it will look like it was mutilated by a bear.

- The butcher will charge you extra for clean-up. It's about $30.

- Your back will ache and your legs will burn by the end of the day and you will probably have to sleep for the next two.

- Digging a hole to bury the guts after dragging the deer all day and sitting in the stand is going to be tough.

- DON'T FORGET THE HEAD! It's a fine if you do as they need it to sex the animal.

- Don't bury the head with the guts and on the bottom, sorting through mud and guts to get a blood and bowel soaked head is not fun.

- Wash up outside before going anywhere public, They hate the smell a lot more than you do at this point.

- The deer will be delicious.

- Use a four wheeler!

- Learn from my mistakes and yours as well.

- Have fun, it's all worth it and makes a great story.

This was my first story and I just thought it be appropriate to share it with you. Further reading will include strategies to get a better kill and become a more skilled shooter and hunter.

The next chapter is focused on hunting strategies.

Chapter 11 – Hunting Strategies

Regardless of whether you're a veteran or a newbie heading into the field for your first time, the following tips will help you in your hunting strategies. It's going to take time for you to perfect your strategy, it's taken me ten years to get to where I'm at and I am nowhere close to being perfect.

19 tips to help you

in your hunting endeavors

1. Human scent scares deer. Use a scent free soap before heading out for any hunting trip and don't contaminate your clothes with any foreign scents on your way to the field. Keep your camouflage sealed in a plastic bag before you get to the field, and put some ground debris and leaves from your stand area in the bag with them. This will help you to fool the deer and smell just like the woods you're hunting in.

2. Hunters oftentimes think that doe estrous is the end of the line for buck attraction. It's true that it is a wonderful tool, but that's really all it is. True hunters don't rely on it alone and it's important to take advantage of a buck's natural instinct of to stay in its territory in early season. The scent of an estrous doe during the beginning of a season doesn't do much for a buck, but they'll still check it out usually.

3. During the high peak of rut try to drag a rag that's been soaked in doe estrous. You'll be surprised as it can actually get a big buck to come right up to your hand. There's nothing like getting a buck to follow your trail completely.

4. Instead of spraying down with odor eliminator right as you get out of your truck like the rookies do, spray a little on and then once you get to your stand spray yourself down thoroughly and don't miss your hat and your hair.

5. When you use a muzzleloader for hunting in the rainy or damp season use a piece of electrical tape over the tip of your barrel to keep it dry inside. The bullet will tear right through that sucker and you'll forget it was there.

6. Here's a huge tip to set up one of the most effective scent set-ups which defies the traditional rule of playing in the wind. Get a long piece of timber or cover with the wind blowing the length of it, or in other words from one end to the other. From the windy end put some deer scent at several parts. After you've applied the deer scent to the timber, put it up high in a tree stand just at the edge of the timber. If you put it up high enough, your own odor should flow above the deer.

7. Always practice getting in and out of your stand before you actually begin hunting. It's important that you can get in and out of the stand as quietly as possible to be able to look at a good buck.

8. Use Google Maps to see aerial photos of your hunting area. There really is no need for a plane of chopper in this day and age.

9. Always make sure you clear shooting lanes prior to the season. It's best to trim during the summer. Smart bucks can notice the fresh cut timber and will associate it with hunters.

10. If it's good to be a little concealed, it's much better to be completely concealed. Blinds for your tree stand help to hide you from suspicious deer and help to shelter you from the elements.

11. If you have a buck on an adjacent land patterned but it won't come over to your hunting area until after legal time for shooting is over you can try to tempt it with a decoy or by calling.

12. Make sure that you cover yourself with tick repellant when you're scouting the area in the summer time and early fall season. Diseases that ticks spread are downright nasty and can ruin and entire hunting season.

13. Don't forget the importance of being able to get to your tree stand undetected by using a creek or a curtain of forest. The darkness will not help you in when you're heading to the stand.

14. Make sure you always wash your hunting clothes in non-scented soap and keep them in a bag until the hunt.

15. Try to make a fake scrape by scuffing the leaves in an area about the size of a hubcap with a stick, but make sure you wear surgical gloves to hide your area.

16. At the end of late season; look around for reopened scrapes in the deep brush. Lingering bucks will rarely head into open country but are still going to be around waiting for the last doe.

17. If you're hunting in snow, scout the area for leaves thrown about an area where the deer have pawed for mast. If there's mast around an area it's a good bet that the deer will be back and you can wait for the shot.

18. After you've taken your shot if you find brown hair with pink or red blood bubbles consider it a good shot in the lung. If it's bright red it's the heart. If the hair is thick and the blood is too as well as dark red it's most likely a liver shot. And if the blood is watery and thin the shot is unfortunately in the stomach probably which isn't a good hit.

19. Be careful when coming down from your stand, most falls happen during climbing and it's always a good idea to wear a full body harness when you're in a stand.

Chapter 12 – Taking the Shot

This is where most hunters find out what they're really made of. Shooting is the most important aspect of hunting there is. If you can't get a good shot all the fitness and tracking in the world won't do a damned thing. The following list is comprised of shooting tips from start to finish.

It's important that there is a balance in nature, making it essential that you learn to take accurate clean shots to help keep sound deer management. Being a deer hunter means that you are at a specific ethical level of responsibility as well to give a kill which is considered to be humane. It hurts to watch a deer suffer and the agonizing sound they make is beyond words.

It's therefore up to you to learn the skill that it takes to put a well-placed shot on your prey. You will be firing thousands of rounds in practice and competition at times and be hitting paper targets from 100 and 1000 yard ranges. As a hunter you will naturally use the same strategies to hunt deer that you do when you shoot targets.

Below Are Some Tips to Help Take a Better Shot

- **Buy a Good Scope** – When you purchase a scope don't go for the cheapest, I already told you that you don't need the most expensive either, but be ready to spend some money on a nice one. You will also want good scope mounts and rings as well. High quality scopes are ideal for low light hunting which is important because one of the most frustrating things that can happen is when you can spot a buck with binoculars but not with your scope. A good scope will also have very precise windage and elevation adjustments.

- **Rings and Mounts** – Even with the top of the line rings and mounts it's important to lap the rings of all your scoped rifles. Lapping is a method used to smooth down the spots of bottom rings to get them as closely aligned or centered with each other. When you get rings which are misaligned they will put bending pressure on your scope tube. The pressure is enough in many instances to cause excessive windage and elevation issues that need constant attention to bore sight your scope.

  The more you adjust your scope away from the center of its optics the higher the risk of getting a distorted image and dark sight picture. When your picture gets distorted accuracy problems will begin and the scope will be next to useless. You can buy lapping kits all over the place and they're only about $30-$40.

- **Tighten the Rifle Screws** - If there are any loose screws you will need to snug them down. Use the manufacturer's specs to set the right torque setting for each screw.

- **Clean the Barrel** – A simple cleaning of your rifle barrel may be enough to restore the accuracy and return it to its original level of functioning. Accuracy naturally drops after a number of fires due to copper build up in the barrel. When you buy a gun cleaning kit spend the money to get a good one.

- **Break In Your Barrel** – Oftentimes a hunter heads into the field without properly breaking in his rifle. Rifles which have been effectively broken in have a noticeably lower number of fouls. It's important to learn your rifle and know everything about it, and breaking in the barrel also makes you better at cleaning.

  To break in your barrel use this method: Begin with a clean barrel and take a shot and clean, follow this step five times. Next you will fire two shots and then clean the rifle, repeat this step three times. Finally fire three shots and clean your gun, repeat this step three times also. Use cheap ammo and watch how fast you get at cleaning.

- **Check the Trigger and Action** – The trigger pull is very important to accurate shooting. Make sure that you have high quality trigger pulls that aren't frequent to breaking.

  Another important aspect is that the action fits the stock properly. Speak with a gunsmith to learn more about getting custom bedding to ensure you have a snug fit of your stock and action.

- **Pick the Correct Ammo** – This is where the magic happens, there is no sure way to tell what the right ammo is without testing. Every rifle is different and each will let you know if it doesn't like specific bullets types.

- **Bore Sight the Rifle** – To do this you will need to remove the bolt from the rifle. Center the target through the bore and then verify that your cross hairs are on the target. Fire a few shots to see how close you are to your target then another for accuracy.

After successful boring of your sight your grouping should be about 1 ½ inches at 100 yards. If you can't hit that grouping consistently have your gun checked by a gunsmith and then spend the needed time practicing.

- **Zero Your Rifle at 200 Yards** – Use the drop chart below to check several popular hunting loads which have been zeroed for 200 yards. You'll notice that with a 200-yard zero you can place your crosshairs on a deer's vital areas without the need for any adjustment. This chart is simply a guide.

Bullet Caliber	25 yds	Drop in Inches			
		100 yds	200 yds	250 yds	300 yds
130 gr. .270 Win	-0.3	+1.6	0	-2.8	-7.0
140 gr. 7mm Mag	-0.4	+1.3	0	-2.4	-6.0
150 gr. .308 Win	-0.2	+1.8	0	-3.1	-7.8
165 gr. .30-06	-0.2	+1.8	0	-3.1	-7.7
180 gr. .300 WSM	-0.4	+1.5	0	-2.6	-6.7

If you don't have a 200-yard range you can see that at 100 yards you can zero in your rifle about 1.75" high and be just about right for 200-yards. Always try to zero when the temperature is close to when you'll be hunting.

- **Stay With Your Rifle** – One of the easiest mistakes to make which is almost always performed by a rookie. It's human nature to pull your head away from the scope after shooting. Stay in your rifle and follow the shot through the scope all the way past recoil and to the shot hitting the deer.

Final Thoughts

You put a considerable amount of time into everything from gear to preparation and tracking, your rifle and shooting abilities are more important than all of this. If you get a good shot you don't have to track, and since your rifle is one of the most valuable tools at your disposal practice with it. You'll get better every time you shoot.

After you've taken your shot and you've hit the deer, it's important to keep an eye on your target. If it was a kill shot, your target won't be going far, but if you're forced to track your target, I have a few tips to help.

Chapter 13 – Tracking the Deer

When it comes to tracking deer there is something I should say this right away that tracking is not for every hunter. There are also two distinct types of tracking. The first of which I'll be telling you about is tracking a healthy buck before the shot, the second is much easier and is tracking a buck which has already been hit.

Tracking a Healthy Buck

- **Where and When to Track** – Tracking a deer works better in certain areas than it does in others. Thick hardwoods, rocky areas and areas covered with moss as well as mountainous regions are next to impossible to track in unless you're a tracking specialist. But for snow covered areas and deserts or other lower elevation areas it may work well.

    The best time to track in snow is directly after a fresh snow fall. The first snow fall over a season is the best. Deer are very active at this time and especially when it's rut. It's easy to tell how old the tracks are at this time.

- **Determining the Age of the Tracks** – When you find a track its best to first determine if it was made by a buck. It's not always possible to tell but there are a few tricks you can use to be pretty confident as to whether it's a buck or not.

Bucks typically have a larger track than that of a doe. You can tell by comparing a set of tracks to other in the area, if it's larger than a majority it's most likely a buck. A buck's track may also drag its hooves between steps and make highly visible marks. Bucks are usually solo travelers which mean if you see a set of tracks which is in a group you probably are following a buck.

The next step after identifying buck tracks is to determine if they are worth following or not. Tracks tend to break down over time and if they're old tracks it's probably not worth you following. Fresh tracks will have sharp angles and over time edges will dull down.

A simple way to tell is to step with your boot next to the track, if the edges are comparable in sharpness the track may be fresh and worth following.

If the track is fresh and you decide that it is worth following, then the next step is to get down low and inspect it further to see if there anything distinguishing such as a deformed hoof.

- **Trailing –** Once you're on the trail of the buck the fun begins. Some general rules are if the tracks are in a straight line he's probably moving at a decent clip which means you move quickly. On the other hand, if the tracks are rambling around he's probably looking for a place to sleep so slow down.

Don't ever walk directly on the tracks; instead stay off to the side of it to avoid damaging the trail, if your walk on it the trail may become hard to follow if you need to go back and bucks are good about keeping an eye on their back trail.

When you're trailing the deer always try to stay as hidden as possible and in as heavy of brush as possible to distort your human outline. And if you must head into open field scan the field and edges to see if there are any bucks hiding in the cover.

If you spot a buck there are two things you can do. If the area is heavily wooded, you should sit back and wait for a half an hour and then begin to trail him again. The other option is a Hail-Mary tactic, run as fast as you can where you last saw the buck and at the first open area you get to stop, listen, and look around, if you see the buck running off take the shot. It's a last resort tactic but could land you a kill.

Like I said tracking and trailing is not for every hunter. It takes time and energy in an already taxing sport. But it's a very exciting challenge which some hunters love. I do, and it's served me well but not every time.

Now for Blood Tracking

You saw the deer, you took the shot, and it looked perfect, well that's not how it always goes. It happened to me, I thought I had the perfect shot and an hour later I was looking at a blood soaked pile of leaves and debris.

I'd barely made it 100 yards when my buddy shouted at me, "I see it!" Unfortunately the buck was still alive and kicking very strongly, he ran and I followed. There was blood all over the ground where he had attempted to bed. A short time after he went off running the second time he was gone altogether. I never saw him again.

I did however get a lesson in blood tracking; my buddy guided me a good half mile through the thick of things before we gave up. He knew how to look for deer, a broken limb here, a turned leaf there and a keen understanding of the terrain and how it was used by deer.

Blood trailing works well, it's tiresome though. But any good hunter will at least attempt it at one point or another as deer are tough as nails.

The Following are Tips for Blood Tracking

- **Watch the Shot –** The better you can tell where the shot hit the animal will give you a good indication of how long you need to wait before tracking. Bad hits in the leg mean you need to wait a few hours before you start tracking the buck. A good hit can mean that tracking can start within 30 minutes to an hour. Observe which way the deer hit and how it runs, if it's limping you probably hit the leg, if it's stumbling the hit may be lethal, and if it's wrenched over it's probably a gut shot. When the blood is noticeable where it was standing that means there will be a lot of blood for easier tracking.

- **Clues From Blood** – Blood is your best friend when hunting and gives the best chance at finding the animal. Remember in hunting strategies about blood types. When you see blood droplets they will have minimal splatter but if they begin to be erratic or clumped the deer it near death and about to collapse.

- **More Blood Clues** – Wide blood trails with a lot of drops mean a shot in the heart or a major artery and that the deer will die soon.

    Blood which is in a narrow pattern means that the blood is leaking from the wound and the deer will be more difficult to track.

    The deer may not bleed much in the beginning and if that's the case it's going to take longer to track. If there is no blood you will have to walk in a sweeping pattern for a hundred yards or so from where the deer was hit to search for blood. Look for blood on everything from the ground up.

- **Hair Samples** – Hair is also a good indicator of where the shot hit. Hair which is high on the body is usually coarse. Lighter tipped hair is from the chest and not quite as coarse as that of the back. And course brown hair is the sign of a leg shot. If you get white hair you've probably hit the underside of the deer.

Other Factors of Tracking

- **Rain** – If there is a storm brewing stick with the trail until it hits, even if you feel you haven't waited long enough.

- **Only Two People** – One person tracks the blood and trail the other sweeps the area for signs of the deer, to many people tracking runs the risk of trampling the trail.

- **Use Paper** – Toilet paper or flagging tape should be left wherever blood is found. Use the items to establish a trail or pick up a trail if you come to an end.

- **Wounds** – Deer that are wounded severely often run down hills while deer that are moderately wounded run towards water.

To finish off, if there is no blood look for anything you can. Kicked over rocks, sliding tracks and if all else fails bust out the binoculars and see if you can spot the deer anywhere.

This concludes our chapter on tracking and trailing, as I said it's not for every hunter but if you plan on hunting for any length of time you'll have to track at some point.

Chapter 14 – Packing it Back

The number one rule is to be prepared. You don't want to go off and make a stupid mistake like I did in the story you read earlier in the book, and if you've forgotten the story go back and read it again to understand what I'm talking about.

Before you even get out of your vehicle make sure you have the following ready:

- Kill tag with string attached
- Flashlight
- Sharpened Knife
- Rag for hands
- Rope
- Blaze orange flag to mark tree where you're cleaning (shirt works too)
- Small pieces of sting or twine
- A bag for the heart and liver

Calm Down

After you shoot a deer don't get all stupid and excited and forget about all the regulations that go with tagging. And be careful so you don't cut yourself with the knife you just sharpened for an hour.

Tips for Dressing

- Slowly approach the deer as it may not be dead yet. And being that it's a huge buck it could still have the power to kick you and cause serious injury. Sit back about ten feet and watch for signs of life, if the animal is still alive take the final shot.

- There's no reason to cut the throat to drain the blood, dressing it will accomplish that just fine.

- Attach your tag to deer securely. Check to find out what tag you have and ask how to properly attach it when you purchase it.

- Take a picture of your kill before you field dress it. Clean it up first and put the tongue in the mouth so you don't look like a psycho standing in front of a bloody dead animal.

- Move it to an area with plenty of room for field dressing and get organized. You'll need the help of a friend at this point or get ready for some serious work if you're by yourself.

- Hang something that is blaze orange above you so other hunters know you're there and don't shoot you. You'll probably want to take off your coat to so you don't get blood all over it.

- Now that you're organized with your equipment ready, make sure to relax. You're safety is the top priority and the deer isn't going anywhere, it's dead. Pay attention so you don't cut yourself, this is especially true in colder climates where the hands go numb.

Cutting

- Cut straight down making the incision from the breastbone to the anus, but not through it, and watch for the scent glands and other internal organs.

- Locate the sternum or breastbone and start the cut from there to avoid the internal organs.

- Cut through the abdomen and keep the knife blade pointed upwards. Cutting upward through the hide helps to keep the knife sharp and avoid organs.

- Use your fingers as a guide and cut between them in a V fashion.

- Cut down and around the penis and testicles or udder if it's a doe. For a buck you'll have to reach inside and cut around the base of the penis and testicles so they can then be removed.

- Cut in a deep circular motion around the anus and or vagina. Don't cut the rectum, instead pull it sideways and tie the intestines shut with twine.

- Push out the sexual organs and anus through the hole in the pelvis and don't damage the bladder or urinary tract unless you want to gag.

Take Out the Bladder

- The bladder is a pear-shaped fleshy sac at the base of the abdomen. Be careful with it because it could be filled with urine and that will taint the meat. Another option is to tie a piece of string around it and cut it out.

Getting Back to the Upper Section

- Roll out the internal organs from the abdomen.
- It will take some cutting to remove everything and tie off the esophagus to avoid stomach contents from getting into the meat.
- Cut through the diaphragm where it meets the ribs.
- Be careful when reaching into the chest cavity when cutting out the esophagus. This is one of the most common points where a hunter cuts themselves.
- If you're not stuffing the deer than you don't have to be a surgeon although it is good practice to dress the buck as clean as possible.

Clean Out the Body Cavity

- Roll the deer carcass all the way over to drain the body cavity. Then roll it back over. It's not recommended to use snow or water to clean out the cavity. Only rinse it out if you've managed to spill any gut juices in the body cavity.

Remove Your Kill from the Field

- For short drags you can use the legs or antlers but for any long moves you'll need rope. If you're moving far you're going to need a sled, ATV, or horse. Another option is quartering and butchering the deer on the spot and packing it out in a large backpack. I don't recommend you even attempt this unless you're in incredible shape and have learned how to butcher a deer from an actual butcher or very skilled hunter.

- Take the heart and liver, they're both quality cuts of meat and taste delicious.

- Hang the deer somewhere shady to drain the carcass and cool the meat down. It's good practice to hang it with the head facing up and the tail down. Keep the cavity open so air can circulate through it. Venison spoils fast if the temperature gets above 40° F, so get it processed as soon as possible.

That completes our guide for dressing and packing deer. Make sure and read the other story earlier in the book if you need more lessons.

Almost done for you, now I'll give you a few good recipes in the next chapter and talk about venison meat. After that we will conclude the book up.

Chapter 15 – Recipes and Conclusion

Deer meat is delicious; it's a delicacy of sorts, and if you want to buy it in your local butcher shop it's going to cost an arm and a leg. There are multiple benefits of eating deer and the following are some of those benefits.

Health Factors of Venison

- Naturally lean
- Iron rich
- Full of B vitamins
- Low in calories
- Free from growth hormones
- No chemicals added
- You killed it, cleaned it, and butchered it so you know where it comes from
- Top of the line meat and taste delicious

Now you know about the wonderful health benefits that Bambi provides. Let's talk about serving suggestions for deer. It can be cooked like any other meat, smoked; grilled, roasted you name it. Venison tends to have a gamey taste depending on what it ate. The meat is very lean so it can dry out easy if it is overcooked. When you use lean ground venison it's important to put some butter or oil in with the meat to keep it moist.

If you're looking to smoke it, I recommend keeping the recipe simple and letting the meat do the work for flavor. A good simple recipe for smoking I use is a can of pineapple juice, a cup of soy sauce, a handful of salt, and if you want it peppery a quarter to a half handful of cracked black pepper.

You can make a big batch of the brine and save it. Just take the strips of lean venison and put them in a bowl or container, cover them with the liquid and then let them soak for a day or two in the fridge. After that you can smoke them at a low heat over apple wood or whichever you prefer for about 4-6 hours usually. It may take a little longer depending on how thick you cut it. After that enjoy!

Venison is an extremely versatile meat and can be used in substitution for just about any other meat. Try it in tacos, spaghettis and as steak. It really is one of the best meats in the world with each regions deer packing its own unique flavor.

Since many of you may be new to cooking deer I've included some recipes on the next four pages which I think you'll enjoy.

Venison Recipes

Rolled Venison Roast

- 4lb. cut of venison rump or top round rolled and tied
- ½ t. each of pepper, garlic powder and onion salt
- 1 can each of cream of chicken and cream of mushroom soups
- 1 onion
- 4 cups milk
- 1 bay leaf
- 5 T. shortening
- 1 C. water

Soak the meat for an hour or two in the milk. Remove it from the milk and sprinkle it with spice powders. Brown the roast and then place the meat in a roasting pan and add the bay leaf, soups and water. Cover and roast at 300° for 2-2 ½ hours.

Slow Cooked Venison

- 2-3 lbs. venison
- 1 stick butter
- I each diced online, green pepper and clove garlic
- 29 Oz of tomato sauce and 1 can tomato paste
- ½ t. baking soda
- 2 T. Italian seasoning
- 1 T. beef bouillon
- Salt and pepper to taste

Melt the butter in a skillet and brown the deer and vegetables. Pour in half the tomato sauce and remainder of other ingredients in a crock pot. Put in the browned venison and vegetables. Bring the ingredients to a boil and then reduce the heat and cook on low for 5-7 hours. Serve it over rice.

Venison Soup

- 2 ½ lbs. venison
- 2 qts. Cold water
- 1 C. each diced carrots, potatoes, celery and onions
- 2 T. chopped parsley
- 3 C tomato juice 2 T. salt
- ¼ t. pepper
- ½ t. savory
- 1 T. sugar

Simmer the meat in water with the salt for 2-2 ½ hours skimming the surface as needed. Let the broth and meat stand overnight until the fat had hardened. Remove the congealed fat and add the rest of the ingredients. Simmer slowly for 2-3 hours and enjoy.

Venison Stir-Fry

- 2 lbs. venison (sliced thin)
- ½ C. each baby pea pod, sliced carrots, diced celery, chopped onions, chopped green peppers
- ¼ C. sesame oil
- 6 large mushrooms sliced
- 8 Oz. water chestnuts
- ½ C. chicken stock
- ½ C. dry mustard
- 3-4 C. cooked rice

Heat pan or wok to 375° and add oil. Cook venison in oil until browned and remove it from the pan. Next cook the vegetables, chicken stock, and mustard. Add cooked venison and simmer on low an additional 5-10 minutes until veggies are tender. Serve with rice.

That concludes our chapter on serving your game and our book. There isn't much else to say except that hunting is a fun sport but should always be taken seriously.

Your first priority should be safety and after that the ethical clean killing of your deer. Other than that, keep this book with you and read it as often as you need to touch up, you can bring it with you and use it as a reference guide as well.

Now get out there and hunt!

CPSIA information can be obtained
at www.ICGtesting.com
Printed in the USA
LVOW13s1346171217
560075LV00031B/3211/P